Everyday Wonders™

It's an Apple Tree!

Elisa Peters

PowerKiDS press™

New York

For Hannah Budnitz and Guy Williams, two accomplished fruit pickers

Published in 2009 by The Rosen Publishing Group, Inc.
29 East 21st Street, New York, NY 10010

First Edition

Editor: Amelie von Zumbusch
Book Design: Greg Tucker
Photo Researcher: Jessica Gerweck

Photo Credits: Cover, pp. 5, 7, 9, 11, 13, 15, 17, 19, 23, 24 by Shutterstock.com; p. 21 © www.istockphoto.com/Raoul Wernede.

Library of Congress Cataloging-in-Publication Data

Peters, Elisa.
  It's an apple tree! / Elisa Peters. — 1st ed.
      p. cm. — (Everyday wonders)
  Includes index.
  ISBN 978-1-4042-4457-3 (lib. bdg.)
  1. Apples—Juvenile literature. I. Title.
  SB363.P38 2009
  634'.11—dc22
                                                    2007045224

Manufactured in the United States of America

Contents

Do you like apples?

Apples grow on apple trees.

An **orchard** has many
apple trees.

Some apples are **green**.

Many apples are **red**.

In the spring, apple trees are covered in **blossoms**.

These blossoms will turn
into apples.

By fall, it is time to pick
the apples.

Farmers pick apples and send them to stores.

21

Picking apples is fun!

Words to Know

blossoms

green

orchard

red

Index

Web Sites

Due to the changing nature of Internet links, PowerKids Press has developed an online list of Web sites related to the subject of this book. This site is updated regularly. Please use this link to access the list:
www.powerkidslinks.com/wonder/apple/